3.25

This book is presented to: _____

_____

By: _____

Date: _____

Dedicated to:

Nana's little lamb.

May the Life of Christmas live in your heart always.
R. L.

Faith Kids™ is an imprint of
Cook Communications Ministries, Colorado Springs, CO 80918
Cook Communications, Paris, Ontario
Kingsway Communications, Eastbourne, England

GOD'S PRECIOUS GIFT IN A MANGER
© 2000 by R. A. Ladewig for text and David L. Erickson for illustrations.

Faith Kids™ is a registered trademark of Cook Communications Ministries.

Scriptures marked (TEV) are taken from the *Good News Bible* (Today's English Version)—Old Testament ©
American Bible Society 1976; New Testament: © American Bible Society 1966, 1971, 1976.

Scriptures marked (NASB) are taken from the *New American Standard Bible,* © the Lockman Foundation
1960, 1962, 1963, 1968, 1971, 1972, 1973, 1975, 1977.

Edited by Elisabeth Brown Hendricks
Designed by Dana Sherrer of iDesignEtc.

First printing, 2000
Printed in Singapore
04 30 02 01 00   5 4 3 2 1

God's Precious Gift in a Manger

By Rebecca Ann Lamb

Illustrated by David L. Erickson

A Faith Parenting Guide can be found at the end of this book.

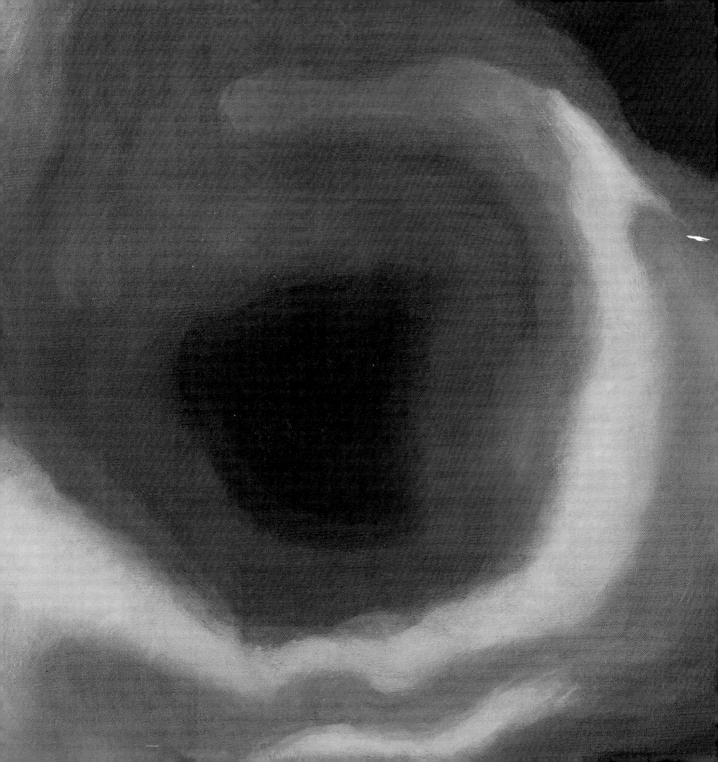

A long time ago, even before time ticked its first tock, there was no earth, no moon, no stars. There was only God. And God was full of love. But there was no one with whom He could share His love.

So God said to Himself, "I will create a person with whom I may share My love. Hmmmm . . . let Me think. He will need a place to live, water to drink, and food to eat. So I will create those first."

God created the earth and filled it with animals, and plants, and water. And in the sky, God placed the sun, the moon, and the stars. With the earth ready and everything in order, God created man.

The man loved all that God had created for him. But he saw that God had created two of every animal, and he was the only one of his kind.

"May I please have a friend of my own?" he asked God. So God created a friend for the man. This made the man very happy, and so he called her *woman*.

For a short while the man, the woman, and God enjoyed the company of one another. When they were all together, the man and woman asked God questions about all sorts of things. And God had all the answers.

Now the woman, when she wasn't talking to God or the man, liked to talk to all of the animals. One day, to her surprise, one of God's creatures talked back to her.

"Did   God say you could eat from all the plants in His garden?" the serpent asked.

"Oh, yes!" she replied. "Well, all the plants except for that one. We must not eat from the tree of the knowledge of good and evil. If we eat the fruit from that tree, or even touch it, we will die," she explained.

"God didn't really mean you would die," said the serpent.

"Why would God say that if He didn't mean it?" she asked.

"God knows you will become as smart and wise as He is if you eat from that tree," the serpent hissed.

God is so loving, surely He didn't mean we would *die*, the woman reasoned to herself. Slowly she reached for the fruit; ever so gently she touched it.

The serpent curled around her neck and whispered in her ear, "See, nothing happened. Take a bite." And so she did.

Instantly the woman knew she was different. *How will I explain this to the man?* she thought.

"Taste!" She said to the man. "See, I did not die as God said I would. Go ahead, try it; you will not die either!"

The man could see the woman was different. Maybe if I eat the fruit, we will be the same again, he thought. So he ate the fruit just as she had done.

Still things were different. But now
things were different between them and God.

Time had barely begun when the man and woman
disobeyed God. He loved the relationship He had with
the man and woman. But now Death had come into their
relationship just as God said it would. Even worse, Death
had come into the world.

"I will bring Life back to the world   through
Christmas," God told the man   and woman.
"I shall call Life the Redeemer." Life through Christmas
will restore the relationship between God and people
once again.

So God got ready to bring Life to the world through Christmas. There was much work for God to do. In the meantime, the man and woman had children . . . and their children had children, generation after generation.

Now the people of the world no longer knew what it was like to talk to God the way the first man and the first woman had done. And because the people didn't talk to God, they became cruel to one another. This made God unhappy. So God decided to go looking for people who wanted to talk with Him.

God found a few people in every generation who liked to talk to Him. And with these people, God shared His plan—His heart's desire to bring Life back to the people.

God found a man named Abraham and shared His plan with him. God made Abraham the first of God's people and called Abraham's family "the people of God." From God's people God planned to give the gift of Life to the world through Christmas.

It was important to God to write down His promises so God's people would never forget them. But many had forgotten about God.

So God chose Moses, a leader of God's people, to remind them of His love. Moses did as God asked and wrote down God's promises of Christmas, so that the people would remember them.

In the midst of God's preparations for Christmas, He found a special boy whose name was David. This boy did more than talk to God—he obeyed God. David found a special place in God's heart.

God promised David that when he grew up, he would be king over God's people. And as king, the gift of Life would be born into King David's family. God told His people to look for the gift of Life—the King of Christmas—to arrive in Bethlehem, David's hometown.

Because it took a very long time to get everything just right, God reminded His people that Christmas was coming. He gave a very wise man named Isaiah a Christmas message to share with His people.

"For a child will be born to us, a son will be given to us; And the government will rest on His shoulders; and His name will be called Wonderful Counselor, Mighty God, Eternal Father, Prince of Peace" (Isaiah 9:6, NASB). This is how Isaiah told God's people that the gift of Life was coming soon.

Now it was time, after many generations of preparation, for the King of Christmas, who was the gift of Life, and the Life of the world, to be born. And God's gift, the Life of Christmas, was His very own Son, Jesus.

God was very pleased with His Son. So He sent an angel to tell some shepherds in a field near Bethlehem that Life had come into the world. God wanted the world to know this King was for everyone.

"Don't be afraid! I am here with good news for you, which will bring great joy to all the people," said the angel. "This very day in David's town your Savior was born—Christ the Lord! And this is what will prove it to you: you will find a baby wrapped in cloths and lying in a manger" (Luke 2:10-12, TEV).

Then, to the shepherds' surprise, more angels arrived! All at once the angels began singing. They praised God with their beautiful song because God had kept His promise.

God brought the gift of Life back to the world through Christmas, just as He said He would at the beginning of time.

God's Precious Gift in a Manger

Age: 4 and up

Life Issue: My child needs to understand why Jesus came.

Spiritual Building Block: Faith

Learning Styles:

👁 **Sight**: Look at the Christmas cards you have received this year with your child. How many have Jesus pictured on the front? Why do we put pictures of Jesus on cards at Christmas? Was Jesus just like other babies? Talk about how Jesus was different from other children and why God sent Him to us as a special gift.

👂 **Sound**: Sing some Christmas carols with your child, such as "Away in a Manger" and "Silent Night." Talk about the special events of that first Christmas. Refer to Matthew 1–2 and Luke 2 for help, or read the Christmas story from a favorite Bible storybook. Ask: Why do we celebrate Jesus' birthday? Why do we have special songs and church programs about Jesus at Christmas?

✋ **Touch**: Spend some time wrapping Christmas presents for loved ones with your child. Explain why you chose a particular gift for another person. If your child has chosen a gift for someone, ask why he or she chose that gift. Why did God give Jesus to us as a special gift? What are gifts we can give to people that aren't wrapped in paper?